T0103566

Soul
POETRY

Soul

POETRY

INSPIRATIONAL POEMS VERSES & QUOTES

ANITA BACHA

PARTRIDGE
A Penguin Random House Company

Copyright © 2015 by Anita Bacha.

ISBN: Hardcover   978-1-4828-5233-2
            Softcover   978-1-4828-5232-5
            eBook   978-1-4828-5231-8

All rights reserved. No part of this book may be used or reproduced by any means, graphic, electronic, or mechanical, including photocopying, recording, taping or by any information storage retrieval system without the written permission of the author except in the case of brief quotations embodied in critical articles and reviews.

Because of the dynamic nature of the Internet, any web addresses or links contained in this book may have changed since publication and may no longer be valid. The views expressed in this work are solely those of the author and do not necessarily reflect the views of the publisher, and the publisher hereby disclaims any responsibility for them.

Print information available on the last page.

To order additional copies of this book, contact
Partridge India
000 800 10062 62
orders.india@partridgepublishing.com

www.partridgepublishing.com/india

Contents

Dedicated to my husband

Yogendranath Bacha FCA GOSK

For his irresistible love of books

POEMS

My Poetry

My poetry is my inseparable lover;
At night I snuggle and slumber with her;
A velvety couch of imagery is our dream,
Of mystic lands, beings and forms unseen;
In the morn my eyes open to her beauty;
In her silky tresses I thread myself furtively;
Her kisses are words of ecstasy,
Burning my skin as evanescent paper
arduously;
As she carves with the pen of immortality,
She turns to ashes my poet's frisk and folly;
Turning my heart to lyrics of past life and
mystery
Together we plough in the pasture of divinity.

The Colours of Monsoon

The fading colours of the rainbow,
The autumn flowers in the meadow,
An unfinished canvas
Remind me of an unsung melody;
Of an impossible love story,
A painful reminiscence of you;
Your smile has this magic hue
Priding the colours of your youth;
The beauty of colours so smooth!
I learn to love the colour red,
Red as the lining of the setting sun,
Red as the petal of the first rose in spring,
Red as the colour of your mouth chewing
betel nut;
I learn to love the colour brown,
Brown as the soft mud in the wet alley of
Mathura,
Brown as the bark of the sandalwood tree,
Brown as the colour of your skin under the
monsoon rain;
I learn to love the colour dark,
Dark as the depth of the burning night,
Dark as the shadow of the moon,
Dark as the mystery of your pleading eyes;
I throw the colours around and above;
I let them go;
The colours fall back with a sigh!

The Little Flower in a Furrow

I was passing by
One morning,
A little flower in a furrow
I saw, peeping at me;
Soft lavender colour,
Tender and fragile,
Flaunting four tiny petals;
A miniscule amethyst ball,
Her belly button;
Mesmerized, I watched,
Wondered,
Chuckled;
I wanted to touch her
With my moistened lips,
Caress her glossy folds;
To-morrow!
I cried out and hurried my steps;
The furrow was barren,
My eyes wept for her;
In a puddle,
Pale, on her tummy,
Lifeless and floppy,
The little flower
Floated in rain water;
Queen of a day, memorable forever
She won the heart of a joker.

If I were a Flower

If I were a flower for the joy of being a
flower,
A leaf for being a leaf,
If I were a stem,
If I were a leaf and a stem to dress up a
flower,
If I were a flower that you will place on your
heart,
If I were all sleek and puorple petals,
Petals to cover the nudity of a flower,
If I were a flower that you will place on your
heart,
If I were the eyelids for the delight of being
the eyelids,
The lashes for being the lashes,
If I were the eyes,
If I were the eyelids and the lashes to cover
your eyes,
If I were a tear,
A tear running down a cheek,
A tear drop that loses itself in the lips,
If I were the lips that caress a flower,
If I were the lips and you were a flower!

One Red Rose

In a valley of red roses of equal beauty,
My gaze fell on one red rose;
I lost my heart and my soul;
I saw my God in one red rose.

A Rose and a Thorn

A beautiful red rose was your love,
Fragrant with magnetic perfumed oil;
Alluring and venomous,
A beautiful red rose with a hidden thorn,
A thorn so wounding,
So sharply malignant;
A beautiful red rose fell apart;
A heady scent melted in thin air
Leaving behind a gasping pain,
A bleeding heart,
Seeking solace in vain.

Adorable Flower of the Rising Sun

I stroke with my eyes
Your glowing beauty;
I inhale your impudicity;
Bewildered like a bee,
Drunk with your perfume,
Secretly I kiss your opulent folds;
Other bees jealously I watch,
Swarming around you,
Thirsting for your nectar!
How I would like to hide you,
Hide your nudity,
Envelop you in my arms,
Keep you like a treasure
Guard you like a pearl in an oyster shell;
But alas!
Blind lover that I am!
Voluptuous, you give yourself
Wildly to the first comer,
Gleeful with pleasure,
Carefree of tomorrow,
Caring for none!

A Leaf of Your Tree

Of your tree so mighty,
I am a leaf so green and tiny;
Neither an apple nor a fig,
I hold on to a twig;
In winter I shiver and I freeze;
In summer I sway in the breeze;
Drenched in torrential rain,
I cry in grief and pain;
Scalded in the burning sun,
I shrivel and I shun;
A creeper I long to mime,
My arms enlacing you;
Heavenly heights to climb,
My soul enrobing you.

In The Meadow of My Heart

In silence I probe my heart,;
To write some lines for you
'Ask the meadow!' Says my heart,
'Ask the flower!' Says the meadow,
'Ask the lake!' Says the flower;

Lulled by quiet inspiration,
These lines I write for you;

Afloat on a lake of heavenly bliss,
On a bed of scented flowers,
Your memory lingers,
As profound as the still waters,
As vast as the meadow,
As nostalgic as the perfume of wild blooms;

If I were to forget you,
I would forget the meadow, the flower, the
lake;
I would forget my poetry.

Fly Butterfly Fly

O Sweet!
Flickering butterfly!
Why are you crying over a fading flower?
For each flower that withers,
Thousands buds are burgeoning;
For each new blossom,
Butterflies are craving;
Spread your wavering wings and fly!
Fly beautifully! Fly lovingly!
Fly to a new destiny!

Spring is Here

With a magic splash of fresh paints,
Trees and plants,
Grim and dark,
With a spark
Into emerald green, are changed;
Donned is the sky in glistening blue;
Splendid and meek, the golden sun
Flirts jauntily;
Budding flowers kiss delicately,
Coaxing beauty in the fun;
As spring plays with colours,
With the melodious songs of birds,
The waltz of cheery butterflies
And, the noble heart of man,
New hopes, like fresh petals unbolt,
Blossom gaily in the garden of life.

Altar Flower

An altar flower, pure and untainted,
Lord! I am praising you for the day;
My fragrance from the sky above,
Intoxicating you with celestial love,
My hues deeper than the bluest sky,
Melt your soul with wondrous delight;
My eyes locked into your eyes;
Your eyes locked into my eyes;
We heaved a sigh!
At dusk, my colours fade and whinge;
My fragrance wanes and whines;
A crinkled altar flower, I do not die;
I merge in you; you merge in me,
As we wander yonder in lovers' paradise.

The Paper Rose

In your garden of roses, Lord,
Buds,
Half Blossoms,
Full Blossoms,
Colourful roses,
Beautiful roses
Flutter and dance gaily,
Caressed by your breath;

In your garden of roses, Lord,
Blown by the wind,
Swirled across lands, seas and moors,
In a bed of thorns, nestles the paper rose.
No colour to catch your eyes,
No perfume to fill your head,
For Your Grace, implores the paper rose.
Trampled over,
Forsaken by kith and kin,
'Et tu?' she beseeches thee
When your shadow suddenly covers the sky;

In your garden of roses, Lord,
In a jolt, you halt your stroll;
Ceremoniously you bend your knees,
Your hands cupping the paper rose;
Listlessly on your bosom,
Drops of tears wetting her withered folds,
Murmuring softly 'Te amo!' in her ear,
The kiss of life you blow onto the paper rose.

Good Morning

I woke up this morning as fresh as a daisy,
Jumping with 'joie de vivre' and upbeat energy;
An avalanche of love pours from my heart,
As I open to the Universe,
Unto its luminescent folds.

The Magic Butterfly

I sit by my window,
I behold a magic butterfly,
A rainbow butterfly!
Gorgeous hues of red, blue, indigo,
Orange, green, heavenly mauve,
Immaculate yellow,
Fluttering loftily,
Flying stealthily,
Flirting with sweet flowers so lovely!
A discreet kiss on the lips of the white pansy,
A soft caress on the dahlia's cheek,
A gentle stroke on the red nose of the poppy!
Hibiscus, violets,
Budding marigolds,
Chuckle and open their folds,
Engrossed by the magic butterfly!
A fragrant red rose,
Spreads her velvety petals,
Lingers and whimpers!
In the wilderness,
He vanished, the magic butterfly!

Butterfly

I am not flirtatious,
I adore people,
I love to ramble from place to place;
Everywhere I go,
Every new face I encounter,
I leave a piece of my heart.

Precious Child of God

When the most beautiful rose is born in a
bed of thorns
And, the purest lotus in the slush of the lake;
By what name shall I call you, for god's sake,
Precious little flower
Born in the muck of the gutter?

Pure Love

Love makes us children,
Pure and simple,
Humble and egoless;
Love makes the world,
A magic play ground,
Where you and I,
The animals and the birds,
The flowers and the plants,
Play freely
In perfect harmony.

Ode to a Pure Soul

O Pure Soul!
The love that torments you,
Fills your thoughts with words;
Words that lie to you;
Do not prefer the lure of illusion
To the purity of your eyes;
Let the beauty of the flowers,
The romance of the love birds
Be your guide;
Merge in the splendour of the luscious sea
As you dive in the pure profundity;
Be one with the candid love of your soul!

Ode to the Holy One

You are born again and again
Like a flame in my heart, O Holy One!
My eyes marvel and rejoice at your sight,
In the darkness you are my light!
In the void your voice is rapturous music,
When you are with me nothing is amiss;
Every droplet of rain is a cup of bliss;
Every thorn is a budding lotus flower;
Every woe is over and done forever!

Spiritual Fragrance

O Adorable Lord of the Universe,
The One who has dark skin!
Thy flute with me,
Open my heart and channel my quill!
Let me engrave the lyrics!
Let your Glory be sung,
Angels dance to your tune!
As from door to door,
Shore to shore
Songs of celestial love are strewn,
Filling ears and hearts to the full;
The nectarine story of Eternal Love unfolds,
Penned by whom thou hast chosen!

The Flute Player

Soft and enchanting music,
Opened the gates of heaven;
I tiptoed out of breath,
In a garden of gorgeous flowers;
Intoxicated by the scent of the flora,
Of all beauty,
I tilted slightly,
Almost lost myself;
Enthralled by the sweetest,
Of the sweet fragrance,
I fell under the charm of the flute player.

Nirvana

Lost in the tranquil water of a lake,
Two fabulous black diamonds I gaze;
Elated in the zenith of your love,
Deep into your mesmeric eyes I rove.

My Precious Love

I awaken to the music of your soul, my
Precious Love!
I awaken to myself;
I discover the lyrics of your song,
I discover myself;
I know you as my soul,
I know you as myself...as my love...as my life!

Apsara

I rambled in exotic lands,
Wondered at romantic faces,
I gazed in the depth of wondrous eyes,
Kissed luscious lips,
I played with scented tresses of elves,
Caressed their moist skin,
But pure love I felt
Only at the sight of you!

꧁꧂

The Waiting

May this waiting draw to a close, my love!
That very soon we are united at last!
In a mad and passionate hug,
My heart shall beat with your heart,
Away our tears shall flow in abundant joy,
Shall wet our parched lips of the grief,
Of the pain of thirsting desires;
That blessed under a starry night sky,
Your breath shall melt with my breath;
My eyes bathe in the clear pond of your gaze,
Swept into the furrows of time and space,
We forget the world, the universe, the
Creator himself,
We forget the intense longing,
We forget the slow suffering,
That shall exist for us only our guiltless love!

Cosmic Love

Your face of love I have seen,
I know what is not known,
Save when you lift your veil;
I have touched your soft silky skin,
Smell your fragrance of jasmine,
You are my joy forever!
May I ever feel your closeness!
May I depend only on your love!
May your light radiate in my life!

Adulation

Your eyes are the mirror of my soul;
They speak in silence
The language of Eternal Love
Having someone to love is a blessing,
Having you to love is a double blessing.

The Flute

I dreamt I were the flute,
Stroking lovingly,
Kissing furtively your divine, sweet lips;
I dreamt you were the flute player,
Caressing my slim, chaste body,
Moving your passionate fingers up and down,
In an exotic melody;
I woke up!
The flute player were I, lost in excess of
longing;
Resounding the music of my soul,
You, my beloved, were the flute
Sighing, moaning ardently for merging.

God of Love

Your music is a brook,
Running playfully,
Singing teasingly,
In the forlorn garden of my heart;
Shrivelled roses, violets, jasmines,
Lift up their heads, wink and smile,
Play on,
God of Love!
Quench my thirst,
Soothe the ache,
Sprout the seeds of bygone desires!

Avatara

Avatara of Love,
God of lovers,
Her eyes swell up with tears,
As your silhouette disappears;
She sits forlorn and mute,
Pining for the magic of your flute;
Your hands, like soft feathers,
Close her eyes suddenly,
Open her vision to your cosmic beauty lovingly!
Your eyes as mesmerizing as those of the
deer,
Lips as red as strawberry in the sphere,
Skin as velvety as a baby's cheek,
Smile as cheerful as the sun at its peak!
Your fragrance of fresh earth,
Golden corn and wheat,
So pure, so chaste, so neat,
Fills up her thirsting soul with joy and mirth;
Rapturous music pours down in a trance,
Beckoning lovers to play and dance

Moocher of Hearts

In the lake of her heart,
Your enticing music
Floats in rapture;
Her dancing eyes,
Her laughing eyes,
Sadden,
Crying for more!

Supreme Spirit

Eloquent words,
Words of wisdom,
Nothing can quench your thirst for Him!
The pool of divine love is within,
Dive deep into your heart,
Drink Him to the full!
Invigorate yourself with His Infinite Love!

Who Are You, God?

I touch your cheek,
I look into your eyes,
I see the pain,
I see the suffering.
You touch my cheek,
You look into my eyes,
You see the pain,
You see the suffering.
I am not your wife,
You are not my husband,
I am not your mother,
You are not my son.
Who am I?
Who are you?
I am the God within,
You are the God within,
You and I are ONE,
We are GOD!

My Sweet Love

Days and nights creep;
I fret and I weep;
I am dying to meet you,
Craving to be with you;
Roads and mounts are steep;
The sole of my feet bleed;
I cannot wait to see you,
Can't wait to be with you;
My sweet dove,
Once you were a qualm,
My sweet love,
You are true beyond a doubt.

All-Loving Soul

The lingering perfume of Your Omnipresence,
Day and night lead me on and away;
Unseen paths, I follow in wonder,
My soul yearning to be with your All-loving
Soul!

Eternal Being

In the silent, starry night,
I gaze into the lake of my soul,
Your sweet, mythical face I behold,
In ripples of golden locks floating lovingly;
Bewitched by the exotic sight,
Engrossed I am
In the sleepy water of my soul;
Suddenly, I plunge in frenzy
To kiss you,
To drown myself in my soul;
Caught in the alluring net of your hair,
Closely you clasp me,
You kiss me,
Uplift me to the celestial height of your soul.

The Eyes of God

The sun yawns and languidly rises in the east;
Morning breaks in sparkling splendour;
The waiting is intense,
Excruciating,
Enhancing the yearning;
Suddenly the White robe fleets by;
Blessed, blessed!
Tears of joy cascade down her cheeks;
Her soul cries out for Him,
Beseeches,
A glance, a smile, a sign,
He passes by;
Ignored, she prays;
She moans 'You called me, I have come!'
'Sweet Lord, from here what do I become?'

He stops! Turns around!
Her imploring eyes are transfixed by the
Eyes,
The Eyes of God!
Glorious moments of ecstasy!
Locked are the Eyes into hers,
Sending vibrant rays of luminous light;
Blessed, blessed!
Tearing, penetrating her soul,
Bestowing the Inner view,
Of His Magnificence, an insight,
In tender memory to cherish,
A divine gift of Knowledge;

Know! Say the Eyes;
Know who I am;
I am in you, above you, around you;
Know that My Eyes are everywhere;
They see the past, the present, the future;
Know that My Eyes are watching you,
Your thoughts, your words and your deeds;
Blessed, blessed!
Your spiritual journey has started!
Come you will, every time I call you;
Your inflated ego will be reduced to zero;
Crumbled to ashes, all worldly desires;

Blessed, blessed!
My Eyes will follow you wherever you may be,
Test you, heal you, and purify you,
Till you lose body consciousness;
Till of the soul you gain awareness;
Like the ripened fruit detaches and falls from
the tree,
Liberated you will be from the cycle of life
and death;
In nirvana you will rise,
You will merge into Me!

A Red Rose

My parched lips touch the crypt furtively;
The biting of the white marble
Down my spine runs shudders weirdly;
My eyelids flutter in bewildered rapture;
Drops of tear fall down my cheeks,
Melting in the dew of a red rose hungrily;
A red rose on your tomb lying silently;
With trembling hands I cup the red rose;
On my heart I press firmly;
A token of your love,
A vestige of the unforgettable past;
The verses of my poetry,
Where do they come from?
The rhythm of my song,
Where does it stem from?
The fragrance of the red rose,
Where does it spring from?
The words speak of your love,
The rhythm speaks of your love,
The red rose speaks of your love;
Of your warmth, your tenderness
Your immaculate beauty,
They have woven precious history;
Is this the end of our story untold?
Or the beginning of a new romance,
An eternal saga of two souls?

Requiem for My Beloved

For days and nights I weep in desolation,
Praying for salvation;
In answer to my prayers,
Miraculously the sky broke open;
Like the magnificent beaming sun,
You appeared showering blissful grace,
In my forlorn breathing space;
Your gentle warmth kissed my skin;
Basked my life with overflowing delight;
Bringing a smile on my face;
Joy and meaning to my lonesome life;
You fed me when I was hungry for love;
You befriended me when I had no friend;
You blossom my budding voice,
When I could not sing;
You carried me in your loving arms,
When I stumbled and could not walk;
You gave me a new lease for life,
When my soul spread its wings ready to fly;
You taught me to love myself,
But most of all to love others;
You taught me to realize my inner divinity,
To see God in all beings;
You taught me to live without you,
To be detached in life and in love,
To let go and not to hold on,
Even to you, my beloved;

You knew you had to go;
Time marches on and waits for none;
Silently behind the clouds you disappeared,
As astoundingly as you emerged,
Without a sign, without a sound;
Between two sorrows happiness is an interval;
Nothing is permanent, you said, except love;
Love is eternal;
Live in love, die in love;
As the river rushes to mingle in the ocean,
I cannot wait to become one with you, my
beloved.

He has Gone Nowhere

HE is here,
He has gone nowhere;
In every atom, in every sound, in every stir,
The Eternal Spirit is here;
Cosmic energy fills the air,
Vibes of love whiz from far and near;
Do not get attached to the physical body,
He dearly cautioned everybody;
You long for the ephemeral;
Detach! Seek the soul which is eternal;

HE is here,
His everlasting spirit is here,
Above you, around you in the atmosphere;
Seek within, He is there;
The Eternal Spirit is here;
Somehow, His call you will hear,
If your faith is steady and sincere;

HE is here;
Why fear?
When He is here;
From womb to tomb, the shackles of karma
you bear;
Take one step towards Him, my dear;
By Grace, the chain of life and death HE will
clear;

To His Abode, you will flock from everywhere,
Because the shepherd is here;
The Eternal Spirit is here,
He has gone nowhere!

Lord of Brindavan

My groom is in bright orange,
I am the bride in green foliage
Singing and dancing merrily,
In the gentle wind swirling joyously;
When our eyes met lovingly,
I shuddered in ecstasy,
My eyelids dropped gently,
The dazzling vision to treasure tenderly;
He cleansed my trembling soul,
With showers of wild tears;
Covered my naked body
With an avalanche of sweet flowers;
Awakened I were to my own reality;
We were one,
Connected together for eternity.

Day Dreams

I dreamt that you were the sea,
I dreamt that I were the wave,
I dreamt that you were the rose,
I dreamt that I were the fragrance,
I dreamt that you were the groom,
I dreamt that I were the bride,
I dreamt that I saw only two foot prints in
the sand,
I dreamt that you were carrying me in your
arms.

Old Friends

Soul mates are we,
On the journey;
From birth to birth,
Old friends are we;
Out of the blue,
We meet and we laugh;
Old friends are we;
In joyous reunion,
We sing and we dance;
Old friends are we;
Time passes by,
We part and we cry;
Old friends are we;
We will meet again,
Some day somewhere,
In another life,
We are old friends.

Song of Grief

Listen to the melancholic tune of the falling
rain,
The sorrowful rustle of the sopping leafs,
The moaning voice of the bracing wind,
The plaintive howl of a wounded hound,
Listen to the tearful song of my crying soul,
Death is what I deeply sought,
Alas! Life is what I sadly found.

Lord of Darkness

O Beautiful knight, clad in black,
Riding a black, splendid stallion!
Your love beguiles me,
Your perfume confounds me!
In the dark, secret night,
My heart longs for you!
Do I hear gallops vibrating?
Do I perceive shadows approaching?
My soul shivers,
Mesmerized by your enthralling gaze;
You hold me tight, in a frozen embrace;
On my back, your cold fingers pencil
Spiders' webs;
A kiss, languid and wet,
Seals an eternal union;
Lifting me up loftily,
Far, far away you carry me,
Snuggled in your arms dotingly,
A bride,
On a honeymoon ride!

Breath of Life

I am Life,
Your lover,
Your mate,
Your exclusive friend;
You won't know how precious I am,
Until I let go of your hand.

Ode to Shiva

Graceful, gorgeous white skinned Lord!
You wear the moon on your head,
You are the elixir of life,
Remover of pain and suffering;
Immutable, powerful three-eyed Lord!
You are the embodiment of light,
Bestower of joy and ecstasy,
Destroyer of darkness and ignorance;
My song is a prayer to you,
My dance is worship to you,
My body is your temple,
My soul belongs to you!

Vision of Wonder

My brow leaning for solace,
In a dream I saw in a wink,
A wall of pastel blue and pink,
Enclosing a mausoleum or a palace;

In a chink are glued my thirsty eyes,
Longing for your vision fondly prize
Bolt from the blue, I see a crimson red poppy,
Petals hanging down limply;

A muslin robe of supple long folds,
Of beauty untold,
On the crown a swarm of black bees,
Are silently resting the poppy seeds;

Nay, the soft curls of your hair!
I behold as the red silhouette draws near,
Your face so pale, your body so frail,
Strolling all alone, waiting for none.

Chains

Chains I devotedly wore,
Tenderly forced on me of yore;
Overly esteemed,
Chains of love lived,
Of carnal sin,
Of sweet give in;
Guarding my fugue,
My getting lost,
Wandering,
Venturing,
In a world of seemingly chaos,
Of sweet illusions,
Fairy tales and apparitions,
Alluring snares and ambush,
Lies so tasty,
Far from the grim reality;
Chained,
I lived and I loved;
A dream I had yet,
A dream so delicious,
Ingenious,
Haughty, I guessed!
To burst my chains,
Engulf deep into my soul,
My true self to behold
And never to be chained!

Words

Words!
Precious psychic words!
Fly me to my love!
Words!
Iridescent,
Powerful, mighty eagles!
Fly me to my love!
Up and above,
Valleys and mountain tops,
Oceans and lands,
Fly me to my love!
Touch him,
Kiss him,
Fondle him,
Squeeze him!
Words!
Awesome,
Divine words!
Fly me to my love!
Pierce his heart,
Conquer his soul,
Possess him,
Enchant him,
Make him my own!
Words!
Infinite,
Invisible atoms of my soul,

Fly me to my love!
Words!
Resounding,
Screeching,
Ejaculating in joyous delight,
Fly me to my love!

Nostalgia

Nestled in my arms,
You doze off like an angel,
Your cheek resting against my breast
Your heart beating to the pace of my heart;
I could stay here,
Motionless,
Watching your sleep,
Rave about the moment of joy,
To have you all to me,
In the stillness of the night,
To me all alone,
Like the moon to the sky,
Alas! The night passes,
The morning dawns,
The sad reality of life hits me brutally,
Awakens me from my slumber,
I unlock my arms in a shudder,
Look one more time at your pretty face,
And, I hold a cry of agony!
I swallow my tears!
I have to let you go!

Richard Parker the Man-Child

Through your eyes of sweet folly,
I found, on a summer holiday,
A wonderland;
A whirlpool of magical delights;
In the woods, birds 'nests full with mint
candies,
French nougat and jelly babies;
Hanging from the branches of the banyan
tree,
Strands of spaghetti;
In the singing brook, enticing chocolate
wafers;
When, at the seaside, you laughed heartily,
Amused that the sand tickled your toes,
Wildly happy that the waves licked your bare
skin
And, with bursting joy you yelled,
I discovered a man-child,
Yielding, warm, whimsical,
Aspiring to impossible dreams!
You built castles on the wet sand;
Sketched with seawater our portrait,
Ordering the sun not to set,
Time to suspend its flight;
You weaved seaweeds in my hair,
Bedecking seashells in the gray strands,
Claiming that they were golden threads,

That I was your queen,
The Queen of Arabian Nights;
At dusk, in the howling sea of Pereybere,
Your body drifting close to mine listlessly,
Clasping my hand tightly,
Richard Parker you made a sacred vow
"The falling star in the sky, see?
I will catch it and put it in the hand of my
Rosy!"
Then,
Why did you leave so unceremoniously?

On the Quay of Farewell

In a covetous embrace,
You gave me your heart;

On the quay of farewell,
You wiped my tears with your lips;
You offered me your eyes;

On the quay of farewell,
You spoke to me about your suffering;
You wanted my mouth to feel your fading
breath;

On the quay of farewell,
You wanted me to remember your desires;
Your thirst and your hunger insatiate;

On the quay of farewell,
You fumbled for the tenderness and
sweetness that are in me;
That you will never find in another;

On the quay of farewell,
You hugged me tight in your arms;
You wanted to keep me forever;

On the quay of farewell,
Heavy as a winter coat,
The separation bent you into two,
And you shouted my name 'Lara!'

The Socks

In coils like two cotton balls,
Coated with dust,
From under my bed,
A brush stroke brought out the socks!
Forgotten,
Abandoned,
Consciously or unconsciously,
The socks you left behind;
Sad, blue,
Filled with bitterness,
The stare blank,
The socks,
I caught in my trembling hands,
Gave me a lump in my throat;
The socks recalled your being there,
Curled against me in my bed,
It was not a dream!
The socks made me a little scared;
Fear the idea that you will never come back,
To warm my bed,
To cover me with delicious cuddles;
The socks made me chuckle too;
Giggle at the idea that I had never seen such
large feet,
Such big toes, teasingly tickling my feet;
The socks revived in me the great happiness,
These senseless moments,

When we both laughed like kids,
Happy to be together,
Pleased that we had met,
Pleased that we were in love!

Hush!

Hush! I watch over your sleep my sweetheart,
Quietly listening to your breath,
As the moon listens to the stars,
The tree listens to the waves,
Hush! I murmur to the grandfather's clock,
My baby is sleeping!
Hush!

The Crying Slippers

Disconsolate,
My legs feeble and wobbly,
I climb down of seventh heaven;
The cigarette butts in the ashtray,
The lingering stench of marijuana,
Laced with the scent of Indian aromatic oil,
My wits are missing you;
My feet slid instinctively in the slippers,
The bunny rabbits I offered to you last
Easter;
I stifle a cry of joy,
You have come back, I rejoice,
Alas! No!
Forsaken,
Left behind hastily,
In front of our forlorn wedding bed,
The slippers are cold and wet;
The slippers are crying,
Howling your brutal departure;
Bare footed,
Your rush to embark the first boat,
Away from me,
Away from reality;
The crying slippers bemoan my loss,
The great void in my life,
A sorrowful abyss,
A still emptiness;

My heart burns in the furnace of sacrifice;
Put off the scorching embers!
Douse the blazing fire!
Settle the scores!
The crying slippers will join,
In the waste bin for sure,
Your razor, tooth brush, clothing;
Of you will be left nothing,
Alas! My wits are missing you

Adieu My Lover

Adieu!
Yesterday ended;
Ends a mediocre love story;
Disloyal we met and left at the break of dawn;
After a night of fiery and impetuous love,
Our love story ends here;
The lover is gone; devastated, the beloved!
We turn the page;
The book is closed;
Today is the threshold of a new day;
The rose that you had chosen among roses,
To be the queen of blossoms,
The rose that bloomed under your hot kisses,
Molten like ice under the warmness of your
breath,
Today, in your eyes, the rose has faded;
A vestige of the past,
Neither you nor nobody will remember;
Providence opens before you, my lover,
A fresh garden of immaculate roses,
A new book of intriguing romances,
A bare page,
Arduously therein you will pen,
A new love story of enchantment,
Songs, limericks and magic dreams!
Remember!
Written with tears and sorrow,

With no hope of to-morrow,
These verses set you free;
Adieu! Be happy!

Disloyal

Impudent, by your side,
I lay in the couch of your lover,
Warm from the devouring lust;
I tasted her perfume;
On your lips moist,
lingering still fresh,
I share your last night intimacy;

Glued to your neck,
a strand of hair,
Here and there,
a hickey that refused to fade,
Mark the intensity of pleasure;

I gently kiss your fingers,
Fingers that have enmeshed her hair,
Stroke her feline contours;

In your eyes I want to know,
to understand,
A call of your soul;
Tears come to my eyes,
Flow gently over your face,
Soft like that of a baby;

In the morning I'll be gone,
my heart heavy,
my steps dawdling;
I will look back once,
Twice;
I understood nothing,
in wanting to know everything.

Woman

Woman! I sip from the chalice of your love,
Sweet ambrosia churned by the Gods,
In the vast ocean of mystery;
Sad is the man, who knows not of your charm,
Sad is he, who has never tasted,
Your celestial beauty.

Listen to the Sea

Listen to the lament of the forlorn sea,
She is calling your name!
Listen to the rhythm of her beating waves,
She is calling your name!
Listen to the sea,
Listen to her beseeching vow,
She is missing you!
She misses your body,
Floating frivolously like seaweed,
Dancing and curving her waves,
She misses your smell,
Deliciously and fondly fading with hers,
She wants to tenderly hold you,
And, never let you go,
Engulf you in the nudity of her waves,
Deep into the profundity of her bewitching
charm,
Rocking you once again in her arms.

The Sea

You growled loudly,
Your hoarse voice I heard clearly;
My steps I hastened towards you;
Halted on the sand still warm,
Out of breath,
The sea, I've been watching you!
Mysterious, a woman you resembled,
In the darkness,
A few stars had assembled,
I imagined your gorgeous beauty,
Gauged your ferocious mighty,
A strong smell I breathed in,
Tears, I guessed, had turned your water salty,
Sated, I turned around,
Ran away to hide,
Returned to my bed to cry;

Dawn came, birds chirped noisily,
Awoken, I listened to your silence,
Walked back to watch you, the sea,
Basking in tender quietness,
Behind you, the glorious sun had risen,
Your hair flowing, angry and rippled,
In a gentle caress was softened,
Hugged like a fond lover,
Kissed over and over,
Lulled you were in his delicious warmth,

Conquered by his irresistible charm,
Tranquil, you had fallen into his arms,
Hushed, you were the sea,
A lost love you had found!

I Dance in Ecstasy

Intoxicated with the elixir of love,
My head spins with the fiery beats of the
tropical drums,
As my body swirls and whirls with the
rhythmic vibes,
The burning sand scorching the sole of my
feet,
I dance and I dance in ecstasy!
Imbued with passion, my heart soars high
above,
Like a shooting star in broad day light,
Falls back in the blue lagoon with candid
delight,
I dance and I dance in ecstasy!
Shrouded in a mist of mirage,
In the horizon I see your image,
In frantic folly I run to tenderly hold you...
The mystic drums stop me,
The enchanting melody beckons me,
Lifts me up and invigorates me,
Fills my soul with bursting fantasy,
I dance and I dance in ecstasy!

The Mountain and the Cloud

Prodigious stood the mountain,
Gazing loftily at the passing clouds;
What a lonely soul you remain,
With no friend, no spouse,
Uttered a nebulous cloud;
Boundless I pass by,
Waltzing in the infinite sky,
In an embrace I hold you,
Caress you, release you,
As I sweep away to another mount;
True your heart is made of stone,
What's more... my heart belongs to none!

Musing

Wherefore is relationship,
When you and I are one,
When sea and waves are one,
When sugar and sweetness are one,
When the soul is one?

Silence

Where do I go from here?
Inseparable as the wave from the sea,
We gambolled together,
Danced together,
Played on the sand a beautiful symphony;
Now you are engulfed in silence,
I am all alone,
Where do I go from here?
Live without you?
Yes!
But how can I live without loving you?
A wave I am,
How do I drown in the sea?

Omnipresent Spirit

The grains of sand tickle my feet,
I close my eyes,
Is it you my sweet Lord,
Filling my soul with vibes divine?

The sea amorously laps my toes,
I close my eyes,
Is it you my sweet Lord,
Sending cosmic waves down my spine?
As I stroll down the shore,
'I have caressed His Feet!' whispers the sand,
'I have kissed His toes!' murmurs the sea,
You walk with me, my sweet Lord!

Yearning for Liberation

You, my Lord, have bestowed me wings,
Spreading my wings,
I have crossed over the seas,
I have travelled over the lands,
Yearning for you;

You, my Lord, have blessed me with purity,
Draped in white silk,
I have walked up the aisle,
Bouquet of white roses in my hands,
Yearning for you;

The bells are ringing in the church,
The priest joins his hands in prayer,
Eagerly watches the congregation,
As I kneel at the altar,
Yearning for you;

You, my Lord, have clipped my wings,
I can no longer fly,
I stagger and I die,
Pure till the end,
Draped in white silk,
Yearning for you.

Meditation

Birds are tweeting,
Morning has broken,
Life is a book,
Each day is a new page,
To be filled with love.

Friendship

Take my hand, my friend,
Lead me to your land!
Let our love,
Be pure and divine,
As we stroll together,
Your hand in mine!

Burning Passion

O mystic traveller!
As a warm gentle waft,
You're in thro' the secret doors of my alcove,
Snuggled under the red satin quilt;
In gentle strokes you caressed,
My thirsty body;
Whispering musical words,
In the naked voice of silence,
You stole my soul;
Leaving behind a sorrowful corpse.

Spell

In the sweet lingering darkness,
My soul pines for the full moon,
And I behold your light.

Trance

A pearl dropped from my eye,
Splashed in my inkpot;
I glance at your joie de vivre,
Your immaculate suave beauty,
Covetously,
Words of love I write with this pearl,
Thread with arduous kisses,
Stitched as one with forlorn hugs,
Gauchely,
An ode to the spring of your life;
You devour with hungry eyes,
My verses conceitedly;
You laugh and you scorn,
Bubbling with the arrogance of youth;
Dancing loftily,
In the forlorn garden of my heart.

Dew

Morning comes,
Drizzling rain,
A drop of dew,
Darling, I miss you!

Reverie

Silently I gazed at the sky,
Deeply immersed in a reverie;
In a twinkle a star fell,
Landed in my arms;
My little angel,
You are the star;
The star of my lonely night,
In the darkness you are my light;
I hug you tightly,
Cover you with wet kisses,
As you sleep in my dreams all night.

I am Love

I close the door of my mind,
I open my heart,
I open my heart to Love,
I feel Love,
I embrace Love,
I know Love as my Self.

Amour

Your name I wrote in the sand,
The sand washed away,
Your name I have forgotten,
Your smile haunts me still,
Your mouth too,
Small and pouting,
Sweet and sour as a ripe guava,
Red in craving,
Your eyes,
Yeah, your eyes!
Secretive, mysterious, impossible to unveil,
Bury the covert affairs that you relished,
Enclosing forever your secret!
Love of one night!
Love of a summer holiday!
As the sand slides between my fingers,
Your silhouette slips away from me,
Disappears in the skyline,
Swept away by the waves,
Leaving behind you,
The silence that is killing me...

The Apple of My Eye

She was walking on the beach,
A long skirt hiding her knees;
Dotted with tiny blue florets,
A white linen blouse flattened her bosom;
Prude,
She never wore a bathing suit;

Immaculate as the sunset,
Pretty as a picture,
Mysterious as the sea,
Smiling to herself,
Poetic, in love, sweet,
A dreamer,
She fell in love only once,
People said,
The blessed day was her wedding day;

A long trail of footsteps,
She left,
Printed in the moist sand;
In joyous innocence,
Behind her I walked,
Placing my steps,
One by one in her wake,
She was the apple of my eye!
She was my mother!

A Mother's Cry

Pensive, I was floating in a cloud,
Distant and away from the crowd,
In the silence of the sky,
I heard a mother cry,
Why?
Why O God! Do you give the mother tears?
Why the rains?
Why the water-falls?
To quench the thirst of the world
Do not suffice?

Mother

Mother is our first,
Our most precious Guru;
She teaches by example.

The Child

For the child that I were,
For the child that I made,
For the child who would be,

For the girl that I was,
For the woman that I am,
For the old woman that would be,

For the daughter that I was,
For the mother that I am,
For the grandmother that would be,

For all women,
All these beautiful blooms,
Full of love and tenderness,
These stars in the firmament,
These pearls under the sea,
These roots beneath the earth,
I say 'I love you!'

Mother of Mine

If I were to pen your portrait,
Yon memory lane paving my way,
Words would fumble and fail to define,
Your beauty so pure, so divine,
Your laugh chased the gloomiest cloud away,
Your tears molten the frozen heart at bay,
Years passed by, your hair turned grey,
Your sweet smile did not fade away,
O Mother of mine!
A shining star in the sky above,
Shower on this child of thine,
Pink rose petals of eternal love!

My Birth Mother and
My Adoptive Mother

Her shiny brown eyes like ripe tamarind pulp,
Her olive colour skin, her long flowing black
hair,
Her cute oval face and sweet, crying voice,
Her fragrance, vetiver interlaced with wild
musk,
Tore my heart apart as I let go of her linen
camisole;
She is my mother!

Locked in her arms, I snuggle, forgetful of
the world,
Throwing my legs and arms in gleeful abandon
I yawn,
Languidly I open my eyes,
Her loving, sky blue gaze,
Her porcelain white skin glowing in the sun
light,
Her golden curls dancing around her pretty
face,
Her perfume, carnation interlaced with red
rose,
Fill my heart as I bury my head in her silken
stole;
She is my mother!

Mother is the one, who renounced me,
Mother is the one, who found me,
Mother Is!
Mother always will be!

My Angel Mother

She cradled me in her soft arms, the angel,
I slept carefree,
I thought I was nuzzling in a bird's nest,
She fed me in her bosom, the angel,
I ate cheerfully,
I thought I was hovering in a cloud,
I smiled and babbled my first word 'Ma!'
She cried tears of joy, the angel,
I thought I was floating in a sea.

Love aka Love

In broad letters,
In small letters,
In petite letters, as tiny as fly's legs,
They twist and dance,
Laughing, chuckling, teasing,
In front of my startled eyes,
Eagerly I try to catch them,
Assemble them,
Write them,
In a poem tenderly offered to you;
Alas! They furtively escape,
L and O, embracing in jolly oblivion,
V and E, waltzing in magic delusion,
Sweet soul, this poem is sent to you,
Blank!
Kindly receive with a word of thank!

Eternal Lovers

My dream wiggles out of the dormant shell,
Like a snail drenched in celestial deluge,
A dream of red wine that fills the lover's
heart,
My drunken mouth finds your soft mouth,
Crystallizes into an evening of dew,
My ardent lips find your moist lips,
In a kiss predestined and long due,
A kiss of flesh, a kiss of blood,
A kiss so divine,
Uniting our body and soul,
Once again in many lives,
A union blessed by the gods in heaven,
Sprinkled with holy rain drops and drizzly
tears,
Precious gems thread in a rosary to chant our
name,
Cheered by the moon and the stars ardently,
Lovers reborn in eternity!

Wonder of wonders

I step in the temple of God,
In contemplation I close my eyes,
Surrender myself,
Mind, body and soul,
At the lotus feet of God,
Praying for detachment,
Salvation,
Liberation,
My eyes sore and dry,
All the tears I cry,
Offerings of cleansing,
Sacrifice of all ties;
Alas! To fall in love again,
When my eyes open and meet your gaze,
Curse or blessing,
A godsend of endless suffering.

Love and Poetry

Love and poetry boast no barrier,
No religion,
No frontier;
The poet is an eternal lover;
His pen,
A magic feather,
Tipped with an ardent kiss,
Filled with heavenly bliss,
His language,
The language of the soul,
Melting every frozen heart he touches,
Opens every heart like a white rose.

The Gift of Divine Love

Nestles in the heart of all,
It is distributed to all equally,
Let it shine with added lustre!
Divine Love breaks all barriers,
Overcome all pains and sorrows,
It sets one free from all bondage;
Open up! Let it in!
Let it shine with added lustre!

Ace of Hearts

My sweetheart!
When in your arms,
I shiver tenderly,
My heartbeats slow down,
My breath similarly,
I forget myself entirely,
The waves pull out meekly,
The sea stops its roaring,
Nature dozes off quietly,
The birds stop to sing,
Time comes to a standstill.

This Page

In your loving memory,
This page is written,
Splashed with colours of joy and heartache,
Unfolding a secret love story,
With no beginning, only an end,
The day lights up with stars,
The night blossoms with flowers,
You are the deep ocean,
You cannot quench my thirst,
You are the torrential rain,
You cannot douse my desire,
You are the end,
You cannot grasp my vision,
You are Love,
You cannot feel my passion.

Down Memory Lane

Darling mum, you were one in many,
Lovely as a summer day,
Fragrant as the morning rose,
Serene as the moon in a starry night,
You were the world's most beautiful lady!
My heart beat, my first love,
My first day of spring!
Pretty, little woman,
I remember the slim silhouette,
The enchanting sweet voice,
Rendering romantic songs in gusto,
For dad, your hero!
Trying to catch your glance vainly,
On him, your eyes rested solely,
Blessed by the Almighty with a baby boy,
Lilly, your daughter, you dropped as a
useless toy,
Desperate to win your heart, in her own way,
Little Lilly drenched in the rain like a frog,
To find out you were away,
At your hairdresser for a Toni!
No word, no hug,
Only the tears that fell from your eyes,
When on your death bed,
I bid you 'Adieu, my Sweetheart!'
Spoke of your love for me!
Gone my beloved Mama,

Came my Guru Baba,
As love story repeats itself,
No word, no hug,
Only the tears rolling down my cheeks,
When he left for heaven,
I bid him 'Adieu, my Sweetheart!'
Spoke of his love for me!

Brussels Revisited

Sunday lunch in a friendly bistro,
On the outskirts of Brussels,
A hanging smell of blubber,
Roast, mash and stew,
A man in an old over-coat,
Others in woollies and stoles,
Silently bent on their plates,
In their eyes, hope twinkles and smiles,
Shafts of sunlight,
Break through closed shutters,
Heralds the onset of spring,
Like man,
Nature too is keen on change,
A new coat, cheerful and light,
A shawl painted with colours, stunning and
bright.

Slumlord

Night has fallen suddenly,
Darkness envelops the world,
Slumlord creeps in on tip-toe,
Beckons you,
Teases you,
Tickles you,
Inviting you to slumber in his loving arms,
You rub your eyes,
You yawn,
You twirl your toes,
Nay! You beseech Slumlord,
Stop your wooing!

Enticing Slumlord!
Invincible lover!
Amorously he grabs you,
Softly caresses your face,
Smudges your eyelids with kisses,
With your flowing hair he webs a net,
A quiescent mantra he drops in your ears,
When conquered you let go,
Triumphant, off and away,
Sweet Slumlord carries you to his magic den.

The Solitary Passenger

Rush-hour on a cold winter morning,
She hurried into the over-packed
compartment,
Frayed her way in between grumpy
passengers,
The engine started, the train moved slowly,
Then faster, gathering speed,
Immobilized under a clean shaven chin,
Her chest glued to that of a stranger,
She could not move,
For a stolen moment, she closed her eyes,
The cool fragrance of Eau de toilette,
The smell of starch and suede tickle her nose,
She felt the warmth of a human body...
A privilege for the lonesome,
An anonymous traveller in the metro;
Suddenly the train halted,
The passengers dispersed,
Ended a journey in paradise.

Rosary Beads

Often we come across a little bead,
Hidden in the smile of a stranger in the
Metro,
In the furtive glance of a fellow passenger,
In a polite word,
In an underground train ticket,
In the open palm of a tramp outside the
station,
In the rasping voice of the newspaper seller,
In the coin that falls from a hand and lands at
our feet,
A bead that has exchanged hands of too
many;

At the end of the day,
These beads are the beads of a rosary;
A rosary that accompanies us every day,
everywhere,
In our journey through life;
It makes our vision broader,
Our life a fathomless treasure.

My Friend

One year has passed,
Another has stepped in,
It all happened so suddenly,
In a blink of the eye,
Did I love you enough, my dear friend?
Did I say it often enough?
Time waits for none,
But love stands the test of time:
God has blessed me with this life,
And with you my friend,
Trust in my love and friendship,
You are God's gift to me,
You live in my heart,
I love you.

Soul Mates

The magnificence of your beauty,
Your skin, as soft as the kiss of snow,
The fragrance of your presence,
Sweet as the perfume of a rose
On a summer day,
Speak to me of the long ago,
The gentle stroke of your hair,
The touch of your hand,
The sparkle in your eyes,
Speak to me of past togetherness,
Of love lived and rejoices,
The sound of your voice,
The beauty of your words,
Speak to me of new promises,
Of a life eternal,
Of soul mates,
Lost and found.

If I Could

If I could walk over the sea,
I would walk across the world to wipe your
tears,
If I could break down the mountain,
I would build you a home of stones,
If I could go back in time,
I would bring you a wedding ring,
If I could die and be born again,
If I could stop time from moving,
If I could hold you in my arms and keep you,
If I could stop my heart from loving,
But I can't walk over the sea,
I can't break down the mountain,
I can't turn back the hands of the clock,
I can't die and be born again,
I can't marry you,
All I can do,
I can cry with you,
Pray that this bond never breaks,
Pray that we do not seek each other,
Pray that we live in each other.

The Mystic Poet

An open wound,
A bleeding sore,
A trail of turbulences,
In the open sky of my life,
A tragedy is my poetry;
With my blood I carve your name,
In the open sky of my life;
If love means suffering,
I love this suffering;
With droplets of love,
I write these words of poetry;
Turbulences in the open sky of my life,
Trail an open and bleeding wound,
Poet, writer I would not be,
O sweet suffering,
Droplets of blood of love,
With you,
I carve these words of love,
In a book of poetry.

Seraph

In my eyes I have a dream,
Who are you sweet woman?
What is your say?
Listen! O heart! To her footsteps,
Closer and closer the steps,
I open the doors of my heart,
I lift the silk curtains,
I behold you,
Your mesmerising eyes pierce my soul,
Your bewitching smile intoxicates me,
The chalice is full,
The red wine has not touched my lips,
Drunk am I,
In your fevered arms you lift me,
You carry me to paradise in a dream.

VERSES
AND
QUOTES

Writing is a divine gift,
It takes the ardour of a poet to bring out,
The more subtle, the more exquisite,
The more exotic traits,
Of this sublime boon.

***

My word is truth;
My word is my sword.
Truth is my word;
Truth is my sword.

***

Live like you will live forever,
Love like you will die tomorrow,
I live to love.

***

As the sun rises in the sky,
And embraces you with tender warmth,
May your day be filled with joyous hues
Of beauty, bliss, joy, laughter and cheers.

***

Love is a flower,
Devotion is the purest,
The noblest variety.

***

Love is not a big thing;
Love is a million little things.

***

Similar to beauty without brain is of no value,
Brain without money is of no value.

***

How can I sleep my beloved,
When you continue to walk in my dream?
How can I dream my beloved,
When you continue to walk in my sleep?

***

Pleasure is an interval between two grieves,
Hence the inestimable value of happiness.
The seeker of Light should try to attain the
    state of equability,
Transcend both states of mind,
Rise to the state of infinite ecstasy,
Where pleasure and grief are one.

***

God made us strangers,
Love made us friends,
God is Love,
Love is God.

***

The real flower is the one that tolerates the
   hurt of the thorns.

***

Illiteracy is the gloomiest poverty.

***

Do not seek to reap the consequences of your
   good deeds,
You will collect only heartaches and miseries.

***

A successful career woman is both pragmatic
   and spiritual.

***

Behind every successful woman,
There is a man.

***

Your Love is heaven for me,
When I enter this heaven,
Everything is open,
There is no window,
There is no door,
When I enter this heaven,
Everything is in front of me,
For me,
Your love is heaven,
There is no window, no door,
Everything is in front of me.

***

Someone may be in your life but not in your
    heart,
Someone may be in your heart but not in your
    life.

***

A single flower can be my garden,
A single friend can be my world.

***

Do not blame the water of the sea,
If it scorches your tongue;
There is no thirst without pain;
Do not blame the thorn of the rose,
If it pricks your heart,
There is no pleasure without ache.

***

Poetry is the language of the soul;
It is the breath of the Supreme Spirit.

***

Inspiration and higher vision are divine gifts.

***

Inspiration is the fruit of spiritual, pure love,

***

Self-realization is the main consequence of
   Divine Grace.

***

The body suffers from thirst for water,
The soul suffers from thirst for god.

***

If love is a sin,
Let me burn in hell,
As I burn for you.

***

The body is the temple of god,
The physical is the purest expression of love.

***

When morning greets you with warm sunlight,
Birds' chirp, scent of marigolds,
Children's mirth and
Aroma of freshly infused tea,
This is your success.

***

Body occupies so much space,
Even when soul is all over the place;
Leaving without end is liberating,
Departing without dying is agonizing,
Death is joyful,
Absence is painful.

***

'What is the secret of your music?'
Someone asked the river one day;
The river answered,
'I would lose my music,
If I take the rocks away.'
Life is like the river,
As it flows,
It strikes against the rocks of troubles
Let us pack up our troubles
And draw the best music of life.

***

We are seeking joy and peace in far-off
    places,
But the spring of joy is in our heart;
Look within,
The haven of peace is there!

***

Love exists for its own sake,
It has no fear,
If Love is your weakest point,
Then you are the strongest person in the
    world.

***

Live modestly,
Love generously,
Help sincerely,
Care intensely,
Speak softly,
Listen carefully,
Leave the rest to the Almighty.

***

Life is a tree,
Love is the fruit of Life.

***

The body is a rose plant,
Meditation is offering the rose of love,
To the receiver, the Supreme Spirit.

***

Love is a blessing from above,
Receive love,
Keep love in your heart wherever you roam,
Love is the ointment for the wound of the
    body,
Love is the balm for the ailing soul.

***

May we never forget Love,
Love that gives us life,
Love that keeps us alive,
Love that is shared,
Love that is unconditional.

***

Friendship connects two hearts,
Binds two hands,
Uplift two souls.

***

If our faith in God
Is as frivolous as a dry leaf,
It will be blown away
At the smallest breeze,
If our faith in God
Is as strong as an iron ball,
It will stand solid
At the strongest tempest of all;
In our chosen God, raise
An unyielding faith,
Faith that will confer Grace.

***

Self-realization is the blossom of
    self-confidence.

***

Lamps are different,
Light is one;
People are different,
Love is one.

***

Don't cover my dead body with flowers when I
    am gone,
Send me a rose now that I may know I am
    loved;

Don't shed tears of regret when I am gone,
Look into my eyes now and tell me that you
    care;

Don't write words of grief on your crypt when
    I am gone,
Send me a kind word now that I may know you
    are there;

Don't call my spirit when I am gone,
Hold me and tell me now that we are one in
    life and death.

***

Nothing is impossible. Don't ever give up.
When you have done your best and that is
found not enough,
Call on the Almighty,
He is ever ready to reinforce your exertions
with Divine Grace.

***

The soul that is present in all living beings is
ONE and the only ONE;
We were ONE before birth;
We shall be ONE again after our sojourn on
earth.

***

Prayer brings man and God together,
There is no special day to pray,
Every day is auspicious,
Every moment is holy,
Every day is a Prayer Day.

***

Grace is available to all who are receptive,
It is the shower of rain,
As it is the sunlight,
A pot which is upright receives the rain,
A door which is open receives the sunrays,
Keep our heart upright,
Open the doors,
Let the rain clean our heart,
Let the sun illumine it!

***

The one who walks with a lion is not afraid of
    a goat.

***

The silent man may not have many friends,
But he has no enemies;
He does not try to surpass others,
But he attempts to conquer himself.

***

Fragrant flowers lovingly offered to Him,
Gentle, silent and meek,
Flowers for the Lord are we;
We embrace the sweet form and kiss the
    tender feet;
Pure and egoless is our Love,
Praise or favour,
Name or fame,
Position or power we do not seek;
Blessed we wither and die;
Blissfully merge in the dust at His Lotus Feet.

**

Love and suffering are in each other's pocket,
Where there is love, there is suffering.

**

Tears speak the language of sorrow,
When words fail to flow.

**

What is Love?
If full of care,
We have no time,
With friends to share.

**

Roses do not grow only in the garden of
    palaces;
In the most stinking and repulsive muck,
Take their roots,
The most fragrant and splendid roses.

***

People pass by the tree which is barren,
But throw stones at the one which is fruit
    laden.

***

Man when he is born,
Comes with a return ticket;
However difficult or easy his journey,
He has to return to his sender, the Creator.

***

Words are powerful weapons,
They can either make or break.

***

You are seeking love,
Love also is seeking you.

***

If winter is not cold, my love,
Snow is not white,
Summer is not hot, my love,
The sky is not blue,
Then my love is not true.

***

Life is a celestial gift,
Live life to the hilt.

***

No way!
People say,
Not made for each other,
One is Eastern; one is Western,
He does; she does not,
He will; she will not,
One is positive pole; one is negative pole,
One is Ying, one is Yang,
This and That,
Chit chat chit chat,
People are odd,
For two peas in a pod!

***

In the heart of every woman,
There is a child,
Crying for warmth, love and understanding.

***

Every child comes with a message,
That God still has faith in mankind.

***

It is in the nature of Man to love,
It is in the nature of the bee to drink the
    honey,
It is in the nature of the flower to give,
It is in the nature of the butterfly to flirt,
It is in the nature of the scorpion to sting,
All are Nature's creations,
Moulded in her own image.

***

Behind every smile there is a beautiful face,
Within every man there is a beautiful soul.

***

Gifted people have passionate thoughts,
They think alike,
Some translate their passion in music,
Others, in writing.

***

Every time I take the name of God,
Your name comes to my lips.

***

Self love is the pure form of Love,
Love for all is the purest;
Learning to love all is like the unfolding of a
    rose;
The rose exists in the bud,
But is only seen as it blossoms;
Every man has the fragrance of love in his
    heart;
He must learn how to release it to the
    Universe.

***

Love is priceless,
Like the pearl lies at the bottom of sea,
Loves lies in the deepest nook of the heart;
To find it one has to take a plunge;
Mere paddling in shallow water won't crown
    the effort.

***

Faith is a divine spark latent in Man;
Faith is similar to the thread that holds loose
    flowers into a garland;
Without the thread, there cannot be a
    garland;
Without faith man cannot realize himself.

***

Self realization is a state in our life,
When we become aware that we are
    everything.
We are God.

***

No one is friendless,
The one who is lonely is never alone,
God is his companion everlastingly.

***

Man is endowed with conscience;
It is a light that guides man to the right path;
But alas! Often man is not aware of this light;
He is like the man who walking in a dark forest
     with a lamp in his hand;
It suffices that he puts the lamp in front of
     him to find the path;
Ignorant, he walks in the dark, the lamp
     dangling from his hand.

***

You can see the stars when there is darkness,
But they are until the end of time in the sky;
You can see the good when there is bad,
But there is forever and day goodness in
     humankind.

Living becomes a glorious experience,
When it is sweetened by compassion and
     tolerance.

***

225

Love is reverence when directed toward
    parents,
Companionship when it flows toward friends,
Passion when it is felt toward a partner,
Respect when it moves toward elders,
Affection when it is drawn toward children,
Devotion when directed to God.

***

I was groping in darkness,
When I saw your light,
I took one step towards you,
You made a hundred steps towards me;
From the bud, I transform into a rose,
My eyes open to reality;
In every one I see your divinity;
In love with parents, friends, elders,
Children and God,
I love you my beloved,
When I love everyone I behold.

***

Love is the first rung in the ladder of
    Spiritual Life,
All the rivers of life flow silently and gradually
    to the sea,
The journey may be short or long,
Strenuous or easy, miserable or enjoyable,
Regardless of name, form, situation,
All the rivers merge in the sea,
The sea is the Universal Absolute.

***

Yesterday is the past,
Let it forever pass,
To-morrow beckons,
Let it forever come,
To -day is the present,
Let it never end...

***

True Peace springs from within and floods
    freely to the outer world;
True humanity is to strive for the peace of
    the world as meticulously as we strive for
    our own peace.

***

The secret of blissful contentment does not
    lie in doing what one likes to do,
But in liking what one has to do.

***

The wise one puts a brake on his mind,
A hold of his tongue and,
A smile on his face.

***

A stream remains fresh when it gives away
    the water that it receives from the rain;
A heart remains pure when it shares the
    blessings it receives from God.

***

Pain and suffering purify the body and the
    mind whilst keeping the soul close to God.

***

God, like a loving mother, loves all his children
    equally;
Man may be different in bodily structure,
    physical beauty, intelligence quotient,
    academic criterion, social status, culture

and upbringing but, under God's umbrella,
all are one.

***

Humility is the true sign of greatness.

***

Friends are like yummy candies,
The more we have,
The more we want,
My craving is never appeased.

***

Love is a beacon of Light,
Believe in love at first sight.

***

Man is divine,
He can move mountains,
But sadly, like the elephant,
He does not know his strength.

***

Can you imagine a world without love?
If love did not exist,
We would have to invent it,
Love is.

***

Love is a game,
You are the winner,
I am the best loser.

***

My soul crazes for loveliness,
Though like the moth,
Oft I burn my wings in the blaze;
Yet for its attainment, my soul craves;
In love and with love,
O Beautiful Spirit!
Let me flow back to you!
Let me never turn to the senses,
Of the illusory world!

***

If you have never felt love,
How would you know I am a lover?
Love is your nature,
Whether you love me or not.

***

I am Life,
Your lover,
Your mate,
Your exclusive friend,
You won't know how precious I am,
Until I let go of your hand.

***

Romantic Love and Spiritual Love
Are two faces of the same coin,
The romantic lover is a spiritual being;
The spiritual lover is a romantic being.

***

Love is a red rose,
It breathes of passion,
It whispers of joy,
Love is the purest and sweetest,
Expression of passion and joy.

***

Do not fall in love,
Rise in Love,
Forever,
Higher and higher!
Do not be a lover,
Be Love,
Forever,
Sweeter and sweeter!

***

Eloquent words,
Words of wisdom,
Nothing can quench your thirst for Him!
The pool of divine love is within,
Dive deep into your heart
Drink Him to the full!
Invigorate yourself with His Infinite Love!

***

The fragrance of a rose remains the same,
Whether it is held by the right or the left
    hand,
Whether it is placed on the altar shelve or the
    kitchen shelf,
It does not discriminate,
It does not prefer one to another,
So is the love of the All-Pervading Spirit,
It is fragrant in every heart.

***

The field of our heart is a priceless treasure,
Plough it with the haul of our intellect,
Let our virtues be the bullocks of yoke!
Let our psyche be the lash that guides them!
Reap the harvest of Love and Light!

***

Writing is a sublime blessing,
An infinite fortune from above;
It takes a poet's hand to enhance,
The more subtle, the more exquisite,
The more exotic traits of this divine gift;
It takes a poet's heart to share this precious
    cache,
With lovers of the mystic.

***

Profundity can be described without sea,
Sweetness can be described without sugar,
Perfume can be described without flower,
Light can be described without lamp,
But beauty cannot be described without
    woman;
Exalted expression of divine love,
More profound than the ocean,
Sweeter than honey,
More fragrant than the rose,
Brighter than sunlight,
Beauty, thy name is Woman!

***

Physical love and pleasure will pass,
As all mundane things follow their course and
    pass;
Spiritual and True Joy,
Will never wither and die...
Friends come and go,
Lovers come and go,
But the In dweller of our heart,
The Supreme Spirit never fails us...
His Love is All-pervasive and Infinite,
Bestower of Sublime Bliss,
He is inside us,
Not outside...

***

The eyes cannot see the ears,
The butterfly cannot stroke its colours,
The rose cannot inhale its perfume,
The sea cannot taste its water,
The brook cannot hear its song,
Your immaculate beauty is not seen by you,
But by those who are close to you.

***

Real transformation takes place when we
    forget completely about our past,
Like the butterfly we have changed from the
    caterpillar phase and cannot go back for a
    second time.

***

Self-realization is the conclusion of
    self-development,
When we become aware that all beauty lies
    within.

***

The beginning of autumn and harvest time is
     here again,
A time when we come together again to thank
     God for all His blessings;
We thank God for the baskets of fruits and
     vegetables from our garden,
To be shared with our friends and neighbours,
Also to be given to the sick, the elderly or
     those in other places who go hungry;
We thank God for all His gifts at harvest;
All good gifts around us are sent from heaven
     above;
We thank God for the gifts;
We thank God for HIS LOVE;
Even the small bunch of thyme becomes a
     symbol of God's Love and Care for us;
Thank you God!

***

Hush! Listen to the Voice of God!
After the passage of a natural calamity, there
    is absolute silence,
It is God's way of telling us that silence is
    uplifting;
It is only through the practice of silence
    that we gain knowledge of our spiritual
    nature and,
Bring it in harmony with our physical being;
Silence is a refreshing potion for the soul,
    body and mind;
Enjoy silence to-day!
Enjoy God's miracle, love and light!

***

Eternal Love lies in the heart of Man,
Love that is unsullied and unwavering,
Love that needs no reward,
Love that seeks no recognition,
Love that knows no bargaining,
Love that is paid gladly as tribute to the All-
    loving Supreme Spirit,
Eternal Love alone can win the Grace of the
    Eternal Being,
Overcome obstacles, however many and
    mighty,
Cure all the diseases of the body and mind,
Eternal Love alone can end the cycle of birth
    and death.

***

A kind word is not hard to pronounce or write,
And, it does not cost a dime,
But it can bring a smile on somebody's face,
It can make somebody's day,
It can change somebody's destiny.

***

Fallen flowers do not grow back on the tree,
But if the roots and stem of the tree are
    strong,
New flowers will bud and blossom;
Often friends, lovers and dear ones,
To whom we are attached,
Sever the bond and leave us bare,
But if the roots of love are grounded,
In a heart that is chaste and unsullied,
New relationships will sprout and blossom.

***

A wife is like a sweet scented flower,
She does not wither with age;
Nurtured with the warmth of matrimonial
    bliss,
Fostered by the gentle care of a loving
    husband,
She becomes more beautiful with time.

***

In spirituality, each seeker appeases his
    spiritual hunger according to his belief.
When a spiritual aspirant takes to writing, it
    is his way of appeasing this hunger.

***

The beauty of a woman does not lie in her
    dress yet smart,
Nor in the way she walks, talks or writes,
The beauty of a woman lies in her eyes,
The eyes are the mirror of her devoted heart.

***

The body falls exhausted at night,
And rises invigorated at the first light,
Whether one lies on a bed or on the street,
God has gifted us with sleep,
It is God's way of telling us I bet,
We are all ONE under his sleeping net.

***

Secret passion of mine!
Why did I choose to write?
Neither the moon nor the stars above,
Can express for you my overflowing love;
Words are in vain,
Nothing can express my pain,
I madly miss you,
Without knowing you
Stranger, where are you?
Stealer of my sleep, who are you?

***

Love has no beginning,
It has no ending;
Your lover of last summer,
Is gone forever;
This season like a fresh flower,
A new lover will bring radiant lustre,
To your crying heart no wonder,
Lovers come and go, all right!
Eternal love is your birthright!

***

Meditation is absorption in God as the only
    thought;
We are in meditation, when from morning to
    night, we concentrate on what we are doing
    with love, devotion, wisdom, contentment,
    joy and peace.

***

Words when spoken are ephemeral,
Words when written are eternal.

***

Out
Beyond ideas of wrongdoing and right doing,
There is a field,
I will meet you there

RUMI

About the Author

Anita Bacha is a Barrister of the Honourable Society of Lincoln's Inn and an Expert in Intercountry Adoption by profession. Surprisingly, she is also a talented inspirational writer and poet.

She was inspired to write her first love poem when she was a schoolgirl of eleven, only to be scorned by an authoritative and orthodox father. She then gave up poetry writing and concentrated on academic studies.

Nonetheless, her passion for poetry, which she describes as her 'inseparable lover', continued to haunt her for innumerable years. By Divine

Grace, in 1978, she came across a Spiritual Teacher, in India. She then started on a spiritual odyssey which ultimately led her to self-realization. She authored and published two books on spirituality and self-realization-The Maker of Miracles (2006) and My Journey with God (2008).

Anita is a lover of nature, birds, animals, plants and flowers. As a child, she spent countless hours and days, strolling in the sugarcane fields or playing on the sea shore in the Island of Mauritius where she is born.

Her birth family having originated from India and a naturalized British, she is well-acquainted with the cultures of Mauritius, India and Britain. Her writing reflects her closeness to the three states.

In 1986, she retired from the Judiciary where she was a Senior Magistrate and joined the Executive, as the Chairman of the National Adoption Council, an institution set up by the Government of Mauritius, to fight and stop child trafficking and other abuses related to children. New doors opened to her. She travelled across the world to attend International Conferences and seminars, to finally realize that life is a journey from oneself to oneself. There is God in all beings and beauty in all things.

Anita is married. She is the mother of four wonderful children and the grandmother of five.

In 2008, she was elevated to the rank of Commander of the Star and Key of the Indian Ocean, by the President of the Republic of Mauritius, Sir Aneerood Jugnauth, QC, GOSK, in recognition of her invaluable contribution to community welfare.